AF252033

Broken no more

Live Happy,
Live SAFE!

Debrah Marlene
5-17-06

Debrah Marlene

A woman's courage to dance into life,
leaving the abuse behind

Broken no more

FIRST EDITION
2005

Book cover and interior design: Yolie Hernandez

Back cover photograph of the author: HISI © 2005

Library of Congress Cataloging-in-Publication Data

Broken no more, A woman's courage to dance into life, leaving the abuse behind – Debrah Marlene

xvii, 117 p.

1. Women's Issues 2. Domestic Violence 3. Poetry 4. Child Abuse
5. Abusive Relationships 6. Arizona – United States 7. Mexican-American authors
I. Marlene, Debrah, 1957 -

Copyright © 2005 by Debrah Marlene
Book and cover design © 2005 by the Hispanic Institute of Social Issues
Printed in the U.S.A
ISBN 0-9771167-3-5

All rights reserved. No part of this book may be reproduced, stored in a database or retrieval system, or transmitted, in any form or by any means, electronic, mechanical, photo copying, recording, or otherwise, without the prior permission of the author and the Hispanic Institute of Social Issues. The only exception is brief quotations in publications.

Fifty percent of profits will be distributed to eligible support services for women and children.

To contact the author:
PO Box 13034
Mesa, Arizona 85216
Debrah_Marlene@yahoo.com

Publishing services provided by:
Hispanic Institute of Social Issues
PO Box 50553
Mesa, Arizona 85208-0028
480-983-1445
www.hisi.org

SPECIAL THANKS

To my wonderful friend Joyce B. Maillard, I give many thanks. She has added more than a chapter to my life. She has been God's truest gift to me. She has entered my life at its darkest hour. I had been robbed of my life and direction.

Joyce has given me much to be thankful for. The laughter she brings into our friendship is priceless. She is an ornament to my soul; feeding me much praise, giving me words of wisdom, sharing her hope for me.

She is the guiding star, she is my encouragement, and she is the friend who pushes me to pursue my dreams. Thank you, my best friend.

To Lori Tolere, M.S.W., in Mesa, Arizona. She was my counselor, therapist, and my sanity. She was always there to give understanding to the commotion in my life.

She taught me to let everything roll off my shoulders and to live one day at a time. To this day I use this wise advice. Lori always made herself available when I really needed her, being a big help to me.

Lori planted the seed of hope, and it's funny because today I find myself sprouting all over the place. Thank you ever so much.

The book would not have been possible without the help of the people who had faith in me as a person and in my writings. Thank you: Sue Morrison (Boston), Vivica Miguel, Helen Edwards, O'Shea, Flor G. Fernandez, Sherry K. Dean, Lillian Kelley, Nancy Moya, Dan Hockersmith, Pattie English, Peggy Lewis, Mark Lauher, Rox, Terry, additionally Jim and Pattie Jones, and Marge Vargas. Your contributions have brought this book to fruition.

And finally, a special thumbs up to the Hispanic Institute of Social Issues. You are an outstanding and professional organization I was pleased to have found you. May we go in to the future with a hope of working together again.

An enormous thank you to everyone once again.

Deb
Mesa, Arizona
September 2005

PREFACE

In April 2005, I read an article in the Arizona Republic about domestic violence. It stated something to the effect that 1600 persons are turned away monthly due to the lack of shelters. We're talking about adults and children having to return to abusive homes.

This was like a direct punch to my stomach, I was horrified. I have been an abused woman most of my life. So, this really hit home with me. I found myself writing new material and pulling out the old.

Soon after, I contacted HISI and faxed over samples of my writings, and here we are, after much work, a finished and published book.

My promise since the beginning was to give fifty percent of "Broken no more" profits to domestic violence shelters in Arizona. This is my way of giving back for all I received in the gift of life from our Savior. Life is good, I am safe, and I'm where I belong.

My Pledge

Thank you for your purchase of this book. I have promised to give back to my community by donating fifty percent of the profits of this book to organizations who help women and children.

Encourage your family and friends to buy the book too. Keep me in thought as I now submit my second manuscript "Much More to Say," to well known publishers.

I AM YOU

I am you –
I grew up poor, not knowing my father, doing without
a lot of things. I had adult responsibilities, I was a child
thief, loud, noisy, I would grow-up to be rebellious.

I am you –
Uneducated, broke, an alcoholic, anorexic, bulimic – I
am now fat – I have had depression, compulsive habits,
stupid choices, all the wrong men.

I am you –
I have been beaten, lied to, cheated on. I have been
conned, taken advantage of. I have been controlled. I
have almost been killed.

I am you –
I have been molested, I have been raped, I have been
abused and discarded for many years. My heart ripped
from my being, my soul smothered to its death.
Yes, I have even attempted suicide!

I am you –
I am an underachiever by most standards.
I have been everything except a drug user.
I am many things, but remember this,
I am a survivor by choice.

CONTENTS

1   SECTION ONE

My Beginning - My Shattered Childhood

3   Her Courage
4   Imagine That
5   This Path
6   The Haunting of You
7   Your Hand, My Mouth
8   My Sadness Today
9   To My Mom
10   Her Words, Her Tears
11   My Mom

13   SECTION TWO

Looking for Love: Finding much Heartache

The men in my life were all the wrong men. It became a pattern and eventually it became a way of life.

15   These Tears Are Mine
16   Breaking Apart
17   His Request
18   I Want a Life
19   Close to Divorce
20   Saddened by the Change
21   Foolish Me

22 Your Affair
23 One Week
24 A Story of Hearts
25 Addiction

---

27 *Section Three*

My Abusive Love

My abuse was real because I allowed it. It was all I knew of love then. It was me playing pretend that all was well.

29 It's a Shame
30 Pain
31 My Name
32 Whore
33 Erase
34 Can't Remember
35 Why?
36 My Suicide
37 Driving Nowhere
38 Somewhere, Someday Came
39 No Plan to Love
40 Frail Me
41 Important Things I Wish You Knew

---

43 *Section Four*

My Heart Matures, Seeking a Better Understanding of What I Need

45 You Say I Don't Know

46   Not Well
47   Not Enough
48   I Wish
49   I Thought
50   Easy Love
51   Holding on With Hope
52   Just My Thoughts
53   Perfect Picture
54   Only Sex
55   No Life
56   Not This Time
57   Knowing
58   Empty Words
59   The Phone
60   Wish

---

61   *SECTION FIVE*

A Bold Awakening

God gives me a wakeup call - He tells me that life must be lived...

63   Me, Then and Now
64   Cry Not for Me
65   A Card or Two
66   Being Alone
67   My Opinion of Love
68   My Need Then, My Want Now
69   My Yesterdays
70   I Want
71   Living for Love

72   Cycle of Abuse
73   This Fight

---

75   *SECTION SIX*

Broken No More

God nourished me with special friends (Earthly angels) and with much love, I write about them.

77   Broken No More
78   Today, I Cry For You
79   My Wish for You
80   Margo
81   This Man
82   Choose to Live
83   My Other Best Friend, Vivica Miguel
84   Your Wall
85   Hard to Read
86   Gorgeous
87   Off Key
88   Angel of Life
89   In Friendship for Pattie English, R.N.
90   Arms Wide Open

---

91   *SECTION SEVEN*

Finding My Direction

The silver lining to life I irradiate all my gifts of His blessings.

93   In the Spirit of God
94   In His Arms
95   Identity
96   Empty? No, Half Dead? Yes
97   A Vision of Hope
98   After the Pain
99   Direction
100   The Hands of God
101   Breaking Ground
102   With Understanding
103   Taking My Life Back

105   *SECTION EIGHT*

Illusage

Rewinding my past, moving forward with tears of joy.

107   Lessons Learned
108   Too Much to Ask?
109   Variety
110   His Words
111   Looking In
112   Crumbled
113   Private Viewing
114   Box
115   Tears of Joy
116   An Abused Persons Prayer

117   A FINAL THOUGHT

My Beginning - My Shattered Childhood

Her Courage

Pregnant and broke with nowhere to go,
she ran barefoot with child in tow,
knowing she'd have to return for the other children.
She was a mother of eight.

She had endured the many beatings,
the humiliation that was part of her daily routine.
This was the price she paid for being that bastard's wife.

God gave her courage to protect her children;
she had learned an ugly secret –
he was touching her little girls.

This was clearly not a price she would allow us
(the girls) to pay – so we ran to safety far away.

Imagine That

Divorced with nine children
a three bedroom house with one bathroom.
Fresh tortillas with rice and beans daily.

Mom, a beautiful woman tired and broken,
holding two jobs to provide,
struggling to make ends meet.

Stress takes hold – she grows tired.
She yells harshly, she yells louder, more often.
Irritability takes over, she strikes out at us.

Demanding more – keep the house clean, do the
laundry, feed the other children, go to bed early.
Keep the doors locked. She was gone to work again.

Imagine everyday to have such a horrendous routine.
All she ever wanted was all of us together and she
kept it that way.

She tried so hard to protect us
from the cruel world - unaware that the world might
have been kinder than her.

She had forgotten to be soft, to be fun, she was too
tired to notice, imagine that.

This Path

This cry long overdue, my heart heavy with burden.
It was you, who started my destructive path,
to accept love in its ugly disguise.

Words of love followed by harsh punishments,
affection given only to mask your anger.

I thought my name was son of a bitch.
How does a mother love her children –
and hate them more?

The Haunting of You

The haunting of you lives deep inside of me.
I was the child you made one of your punching bags.

I became your weekly exercise,
you and your big belt swinging hard at me.

Growing older, my tongue sharp as scissors,
my attitude was all about you.

I refused to let you break me, so I endured the twig, the
flyswatter, the pinching, your pulling my hair, that
extension cord leaving welts on my legs.

Then came the slaps, all ten in a row –
you were still the bitch.

I was now a teen and your misuse of me made me a
survivor and a victim of much to come.

Your Hand, My Mouth

Your hand slaps hard against my mouth: often, daily.

I had too many questions:
Why do I have to wash that pail of dirty diapers?
Why do I have to wash, wring, hang, and fold them?
Why do I have to change soiled diapers?

I'm not the mom – you slap me.

Why do I have to make sure he stops crying?
I can't even stop myself from crying.

I was only a little girl myself!
You made me grow up too fast
to really enjoy life as a child.

Your hand and your grown up demands.

My Sadness Today

Today I feel sadness
my mom would be reading my poetry.
Poetry that does not flatter her.

It is my truth as to how she
brought me up.

I wonder if she would deny my punishments?
Maybe she wouldn't remember –
like a selective memory well practiced.

Would we have an exchange of words
that would hurt us?

Would she make me feel like the little girl
again with her tongue that bites?

Would she try to chew me up and spit me out?

And, discard me like a bad taste in her mouth?

My sadness is real today, old feelings surface
because there are some things I can't forget!

To My Mom

This writing has nothing to do with you,
it is all about me.

It is about my process to grow, to go forward,
to heal all my hurts.

It is about me jumping into life with explosion – I want
to be like a fire cracker overpowering the night sky.

It is about me being your angel and forgiving.

It is about giving you "thanks" for doing the best you
could under your circumstances.

It is about me embracing you now with much
understanding.

Her Words, Her Tears

Her words I heard as if she were yelling.
I heard a broken woman not sure what to make
of an expressive daughter.
I had hurt her with poetry.

Her tears I could see
as if she were sitting across from me –
the telephone hid nothing.

Her anger I had grown accustomed to.
I would never get used to her face with streaks of pain
from tears I caused with no intent.

Words to send me on my final journey –
to healing, open the skeleton door for her.

Her words, her tears,
I carry with me everywhere I go.
They take residency in my heart.
She's my mom – how can I not care?
I love her more than she knows.

My Mom

In the wrinkles on her face are adventures never lived.
In the grey of her hair are stories to tell.
Her eyes lack spark; life has been hard, her hands
coarse, like those of a man.

She has been my mother – my father.
Doing it all alone – raising her family;
working to the bone.

My mom's struggles are real.
She chooses to challenge life.
God gives her strength to go on.

Disappointed with me – with my writings that tell it like
I remember, meant to hurt no one.
I want to park understanding in everybody's heart.

My message is this abuse hurts long after it takes place.
It lingers longer than necessary.
I choose to live happy; this I get from my mom.

LOOKING FOR LOVE: FINDING MUCH HEARTACHE

The men in my life were all the wrong men. It became a pattern and eventually it became a way of life.

These Tears Are Mine

These tears are mine, don't ask why.
Please don't prey.

Emotions too deep to share,
because you wouldn't understand
what love has done to me.

Let me have my moments.
With time, I'll be all right.

Breaking Apart

Being lied to isn't what I want.

Falling to pieces, crazy with emotion
isn't what I need.

The feeling of your detachment is hard.

Falling down with disappointment isn't
what I hope for.

The breaking of my heart is often –
breaking I cry.

You have given me the final shove.

His Request

"Come home I need you with me"
and here I sit alone again.

In and out for booze or a better laugh
because God knows we don't laugh anymore.

What's the use?
You're tired of me and I can't withstand the
embarrassment of your choice of friends.
And who knows, what has gone on in my absence?

The joke is on me - I know.

This shame is real.

I Want a Life

I need of someone to talk to who really cares to listen.

I want to share the personal depths of my inner self
with someone who might love me.

Not knowing how to let go of all my pain,
I cry often - realizing I do want my life to be more.

What I have now is not a life.

Close to Divorce

When a man tires of a woman,
he should just walk out,
leave the relationship.

This tug of war has gone on too long.
There should be no more lies.
Dare to tell it like it is.

Your awful truth would make more sense,
than this constant fight.

I can handle realism.
Can you?

Saddened by the Change

Feeling sad about my change of heart,
I wish I were blind and deaf
so that I may not see and hear your anger.

This is not the first time you have broken my happy
spirit – the torment is real because of your rage.

The time is now to put our shared life behind us.

I feel no tomorrow could lead us anywhere important.

You did this to us!

Oh, what might have been!

Foolish Me

I left work knowing I'd be free of responsibilities.

I sold all I owned to run off to the east with him.

He, who said he loved me,
and I knowing I loved him more!

I took a chance at love.

A love I wanted to work.

Alone with time passing,
I wonder if that was my last chance?

Your Affair

You said it was nothing.

"What is wrong with it?"
You dare to ask.

You must feel my absence by now.

I'm wondering if you realize that your affair
was indeed something to me.

One Week

One week short of a year
that I ran from your abusive ways.

Fifty-one weeks that I still love you.

Maybe next year will bring me a loss of memory,
so that I might learn to go on.

A Story of Hearts

This heart should know better.
It had its broken promises before.

This heart needs to love - wants you again.
Emotional needs dominated all sense concerning love.

You made the call, wanting me!
Needing me to fill your emptiness.

This heart thought you were for real.
Your heart never told mine that it was just kidding.

This heart is hurting again.

Addiction

I always believed that you'd come back and love me.

I knew you loved me,
but not more than your drugs;
it was an addiction –
like I to you.

You were my Knight in Shining Armor; then you died.

MY ABUSIVE LOVE

My abuse was real because I allowed it.
It was all I knew of love then.
It was me playing pretend that all was well.

It's a Shame

It's a shame you couldn't look beyond this fat body.
You might have gotten close enough
to this heart that pumps hard with emotion.
A heart full of love for you.

I cried, your words echo in my mind:
"'Fat bitch', 'slut', 'pig'
'Just get out of my life'"!

I wish I'd known you hated my being.
I would have let go of this relationship so much sooner.

It's a shame that you thrived on hurting me.
The meaning of your words
will keep me away like a sudden death.

Pain

Pressure and hurt.

Alive and wishing I were dead.

Impossible to bare.

Never really gone.

My Name

She calls me
La Debrah –
like he used to so long ago.
A man not yet forgotten,
because she won't stop calling me
La Debrah.

I hate it.
Like I hated,
when he'd slap me hard into reality.

Whore

"Whore!" echoes in my memory like an old dream.
He had referred to me as a whore.

In his drunkenness I had heard the word before.
But that day was different.

He was sober and I was the whore again, and all the
excuses to blame the drinking were gone.

Erase

If I could eradicate this pain I would.
Hurt you planted in me with your soiled anger.
Your words echo, you called me a *cunt*.

I wish all of this would wither and die.
I am no longer a flower.
You made me an ugly weed in your garden of hell.

I am not your *cunt*!
Eradicate that from your mind.

Can't Remember

I can't remember
the last time you seemed happy to see me,
when you have expressed love for me.

I do remember
your anger with your uncaring words
intended to hurt me.

I can feel
that last slap,
because it was so full of hate.

Why?

Why did you stop loving me?

When did you stop needing me?

Why do you love grabbing me by the neck?

Did I stop breathing?

Did I turn blue?

Why did you call 911?

Who were you to decide I wouldn't die?

You coward!

My Suicide

Here I lay in the hospital bed –
people around –
me fighting to live.

I lay here just wanting to die.

I have important things to do.
I just can't lay here.
Remove this restraint!

I want to stop this pain.

Doesn't anyone understand
my need to leave this hell
that's supposed to be my home?

Why did you intervene?
Death was my easy way out.

Driving Nowhere

Driving nowhere was better than staying there.
I was crying, lost in my grief, I just had to leave.

Driving nowhere may not make much sense.
But to me; it meant everything.

A short escape; a time to gather my thoughts.
Driving cleared my mind.

Driving nowhere never erased my pain.
It did make me question: why I'd bother to go back?
The truth was: I didn't have anywhere else to go.

Driving nowhere, I found myself in those abusive arms
believing he wouldn't hit me again.

Wouldn't it be great if my driving nowhere would lead
me somewhere, someday?

Somewhere, Someday Came

Today I realized I had had enough;
driving to work I knew I wouldn't be driving back;
not home anyway.

Somewhere, someday came,
I made a choice to leave and never return.

All I had were the clothes on my back
and my toothbrush in my purse.

Driving assured my choice;
I felt a peaceful sense of direction
for the first time in years.

So I wound up at my sisters,
my friends, a co-worker, a motel.
All of this was better than returning home.

Somewhere, someday, didn't come soon enough.
I'm just happy it came that day.

No Plan to Love

I had no plan to love,
my body may have been more than willing,
but this heart and mind were not.

Today I realize,
I could fall madly in love with you.
Feeling foolish because I knew
I wouldn't allow this to happen.

You made me laugh and fed me all your charm;
so much that I had almost forgotten
my reasons for being alone.

A past lover hurting me, so close to killing me.
Literally trying to put an end to my being!

No plan to love, not now.

Frail Me

The loves in my life were few
and all so much alike.

All wanting more than
they wanted to give.

Expecting to rob me
of all that attracted them to me.

Time passes with no one
because I let them break my trust.

Who would want me now
frail, and afraid to love?

Important Things I Wish You Knew

I loved you the last time I was with you –
the day before Thanksgiving.

The day before my birthday,
I planned a wonderful night with you
and found you gone –
I died that night.

When I located you in Mexico,
my heart was torn
because of the distance between us.

You spoke your hearts truth –
ugly, terrible words to make me suffer –
you said so yourself.
That night you died to me.

But death lives on
because your absence haunts me
like you will never know.

You've got my heart in the palm of your hand
and you don't even know it.

My Heart Matures, Seeking a Better Understanding of What I Need

You Say I Don't Know

You say I don't know of love; you're wrong.
It's because I do know of love that I choose to go
in the opposite direction.

I need to be safe, feel at ease. I need comfort!

I know enough to know what you don't make me feel.
If you made me feel complete,
I wouldn't hunger for more.

I know that love can be beautiful,
it comes from the heart and soul.
It must come from two.

Affection is a token of what one feels for someone.

You haven't given me that token;
will it ever come my direction?

The patience of waiting will kill me slowly.
I choose to die now quickly and easily – alone.

Not Well

My soul is not well, slivers of hurt
that multiply into arrows of pain.

I took a walk only to sadden my life.
I won't play pretend.

I miss the laughter of our togetherness.
My body hungers for your touch.

Needing the silence of sweet pleasures we shared.
Wanting adventures that would have come.

I miss you.
I need you.

But I needed more
than you were willing to give.

Not Enough

Making love isn't enough, making me laugh means
more. Telling your friends I'm yours isn't cool
when you've never told me.

Having women in your home when you're expecting
me bothers me. I feel cheated of moments that should
be ours. What you give me isn't enough.

I remember the first time we were together I told you I
was lonely. I'd be better off if we would have had a
one night stand. My heart hurts!

Today I'm lonelier than the night I met you. Only
because somehow we have managed to grow close, I'm
sure I love you. But I know there's something lacking.

I'm falling – but maybe not in love.

I fear the fall, so sure I'll crack or break.

I don't like the hurt you bring me.

I don't like what you've taken from me.

I've lost my relaxed mind, my happy spirit.

I'm afraid I'll lose me to you, then what?

I need more only because you don't care enough.

I Wish

I wish that when I first met you I would have said no.

I wish we would have taken time to become friends,
instead of lovers.

I wish I was a lousy lover, maybe I'd stand a chance that
you'd want me for companionship and for the laughter
of just being together.

Maybe our relationship would grow stronger
on a mental level.

If only you understood the difference between
love and want.

I wish I didn't love you.
Then I wouldn't feel so lonely in your absence.

Wishing isn't going to give me the love I need.

So, I wish you well.

I Thought

I thought I'd survive without you.
I thought I could laugh you off.

I thought I'd erase you from my mind.
Well, I thought wrong.

I wanted to indent your life by my absence,
instead, I indented mine.

I was so sure I had enough of you.
I was so sure, I realized I was wrong.

I wanted to conquer love.
In need of quest, I gave you up.

I lost.
Somehow, in losing you, I even lost me.

Easy Love

The lovemaking came easy.
The laughter was just as nice.
Soft words, romantic gleams,
honest words with different meanings.

We were so out of tune and still we gave in
to the mood of the night.
Fulfilling an appetite and still lacking.

There are other parts of me that need to be touched.
Touch my soul, indent my heart.
Win me over with honest eyes, and no lies.

Holding on With Hope

In your presence I realize you have let go.
But, I hold on with hope.

Loving you who wants no part of me.

Your lack of words tell me – it never mattered
because emotion is to powerful for silence.

I will love you until my love turns into an empty love
and I lose the state of being in love.

Just My Thoughts

I never thought we'd end up like this,
your infidelity driving me insane;
so much that I cheated too.

Is this what brokenness does?
My love forgave your cheating.
Your lack of love can't forgive mine.

Perfect Picture

I was honest,
so proud to share
all that would be important
to any man.

I didn't try to paint
any perfect pictures.
You did that on your own.

Only Sex

The sex was raw, as great as the last time.
I might have had it.
He was fine.

Not one I would build friendship with.
Feeling just ok because, God knows,
I wondered if I'd ever be sexual again.

Knowing it happened for the wrong reasons,
made me realize,
why I often said no and meant it.

No Life

Living my life to no degree,
I want sometimes to just die.

My work keeps me busy
and leaves no time for fun.

I'll change that.
You just wait and see!

Not This Time

I have been known to fall quickly and easily.

I could take our friendship and create illusions,
but I hold back with my emotions.

I wish not to be ill fated – not this time.

Knowing

Knowing that I was the one to leave,
makes nothing easy.

Realizing I always ran in a rush to safety,
only sure that staying would hurt me more.

Eighteen months later, I dare to wonder.
Because I do hurt without you.

Empty Words

An exchange of words
that have no true meaning.

Words of hope coming from him,
knowing he had it good with me.

With all that he says,
he has nothing to offer me.

I wish he'd move on –
to the next fool on his list of maybes.

The Phone

The phone rings.
Knowing it is he from my past, I let it ring.

Knowing there is no more to be said and still I find
myself missing his soft words that have no meaning.

Only because there is no one charming me now!

Wish

Falling in and out of love is not my style.

I wish I could fall deep into the passion
of an unknown fleshy being.
So that maybe I'd finalize my last departure.

But still, I hold on to my yesterdays.

A Bold Awakening

God gives me a wakeup call –
He tells me that life must be lived...

Me, Then and Now

My writing was me, then.

A lost desperate girl,
looking for love for the wrong reasons,
needing to feel complete.

Young emotion expressed,
always lonely and needy.
A time never forgotten.

My poetry tells a story of past mistakes.
I had no inclination as to who I'd grow to be.
Strong, capable, independent me.

Cry Not for Me

Cry not for me.
Not today.

My tears are a hundred years ago –
my darkness long gone.

There is much color in my life.
My rainbow is bright with much to offer – wonderful
friendships, love of work, peace of mind,
gifts of the elderly.

Cry not for me.
Not today.

There is much laughter, more joy,
than I ever thought possible.

Life throws me a stone and I easily throw it back –
I am unstoppable – I am strong,
I dance with my happy life.

Cry not for me.
Not today!!

A Card or Two

Life has dealt me a card or two, usually jokers.
I was always dealt a losing hand.

Today I possess the cards, I hold a full deck.
The King, Queen, and Aces are all on my side.

I am in control of the game because I have made a
conscious choice to take my power back.

I will never be at the losing end of any game,
I have a master plan – to live, love, and fight harder
than I have in the past.

To allow no Full House to beat me
since I hold all the aces.

Being Alone

My being alone is apparent,
I didn't choose it.
It chose me.
I live productive, busy and happy.

My being alone doesn't mean lonely, intimacy gone.
A gentle kiss almost forgotten.
Soft caressing- a past story,
definitely not a fairytale.

Being alone keeps harsh words away,
fights at a stand still.
Alone offers no algo.
I am safe from harms way.

My grand prize for this way of life is being alive.

My Opinion of Love

Love comes like a gentle breeze.
It brings life to the stillness of one.

Interest must be of two – like a pair of dice.
Willingness must convene like a good read.

Passion must take part like food to a man's heart.

Faith needs to live in the soul like a bold Sunday
sermon.

Love needs strength.
Like a strong umbrella, it must endure the rain.

Loyalty needs to exist so love does not go astray.
Forgiveness for life's many mistakes.

Truth must be more than conviction to keep love alive.
Or a draught could come and take it all away.

My Need Then, My Want Now

A drop dead gorgeous body.
A lot bold, a bit conceited.
He had to have passion for me to be interested.

I needed some kick in a relationship,
an occasional fight – so I'd have my nude glory
with extra lovemaking.

It was these makeup sessions I lived for.
The I'm sorry(s) I won't do it again.
Glorious sex. It was all B.S.

Today I want so much more:
good conversation, respect, friendship.

A not so sexy guy,
a man who is more than comfortable with himself.
And yes, a man who'd be happy to have me as I am.

I'm not twenty years ago.
I'm in the now - with the hope of tomorrow.

My Yesterdays

Holding on to my yesterdays
kept me alive in my past.

My yesterdays were mine.
That is all I've had for a decade.

I held on to the memory of you –
the love, the fun, the sex that was more than wow!

Today I realized I held on to the pain
of all you did to me.

My yesterdays were real, it was my existence –
my shameful secret.

I kept it like my identity.
Today I surrender it all.

You will not be who I am.
You are old yesterday.

I choose to live for now and my many tomorrows.
The future is mine!

I Want

I want love backed with trust.

I want trust given with honesty.

I need honesty from the heart.

I need love given with conviction.

Then I will need nothing more.

Living for Love

I listen to words that have so little to offer.
Words of passion, lacking foundation.

We speak of reconciling,
only to rebuild a trust already broken.

Why now?
When we have already adjusted to
the loneliness of the night.
And the silence of being alone.

I wish not to play.
My life has much more to offer than a game.

I care not to settle for less than love, for love is the
ultimate reason for my living.

Cycle of Abuse

Did I choose not to have children
to stop the cycle of abuse?

My answer would have to be: Yes.

I wanted a money-back guarantee
and with men no such a thing exists.

I wanted love for keeps
and I learned that love keeps no one –
why would it start with me?

I hungered for a fairytale life,
but I didn't even own a book with a happy ending.

At forty-six, I realized
I didn't put an end to the cycle of abuse –
I just put a halt to it.

I have not gone forward with love
in fear that the cycle would return

This Fight

I was my own worst enemy.
I knew I didn't deserve love.
I may have needed it, but for me to believe I was
worthy of love was a farce.

Enduring the many hurts, the pain was what I knew.
I knew not how to break this vicious cycle.
I contributed to the fights – pushing all your buttons.

Wanting to win this fight for survival.
Wanting my need to love, to be loved.

I threw in the towel –
many years later I realize –
I did win the fight.

I am alive and well and thriving!

Broken No More

*God nourished me with special friends
(Earthly angels) and with much love,
I write about them.*

Broken No More

Time heals old pain, mends broken hope.
Hope thrives from the sunlight.
Broken no more has meaning – strength.

A woman alive, after the cyclone of events
that almost puts an end to her life.
Strength pulls her through the tornado,
the earthquakes and the hurricane.

Crying in a flood of tears she swims to shore
to be dried out like an alcoholic needing recovery.
Finding strength to go on – to exist – to now live.

Broken no more.

Today, I Cry For You

Today, I cry for you, a little boy now a grown man.
A little boy sleeps soundly to be awakened by his
mother to be told:
"Mark, I don't love you anymore."

A boy left in the dark, in a bed with much comfort
before she entered the room.
A boy now bewildered – words to leave any child
awake – feeling more than alone.

Today I cry for you, your lack of love for your mother
I understand totally, your need to please,
your inability to say no.
Is this your hunger for acceptance?

Today I cry for you, a man not knowing your worth,
your value, lugging around those words:
"Mark, I don't love you anymore."

My Wish for You

That you encounter a beautiful smile,
a lady with enchanting eyes meant just for you.

Someone with a gentle heart and laughter
that comes from deep within.

May she lend a good ear, own a quick wit.

May she have perky breasts,
slender legs, and a tight behind.
A body that invites you to touch her.

Most of all, may she possess
a little of the cherished women from your past.

Like a cup of good coffee,
may she be your perfect blend.

I wish this for you my friend.

Margo

She comes to my defense as if I were still a little girl.
She takes charge more than willing to protect me.

In school the children laughed at us,
our clothes we shared, our hair un-kept.
Shoes with holes, it was okay
because we had each other.

Margo, one year older than I played mother.
She'd demand fairness and stood-up to authority.

We are now close to fifty and nothing changes.
She still stands strong to defend me
because she is my friend;
my sister; playing role of mother.
Taking the lead of love, nurturing me.

This Man

I was in a bad situation, looking for an easy way out.
I thought I'd stay for a few months; I stayed for six
years because of this man, Dave.

I found a job, a nice home with security and peace.
I found unconditional love with a true understanding
of a family life, all because of this man.
I didn't only find a job, I found Dave!

I found this man hungry to nurture my being,
showing me love and respect
with hugs that came from his open and loving heart.

Years have passed and I realize I was the hungry one.
I was starving for the love this man had to give.
This man gave me understanding to many of life's
treasures and taught me how to deal with my pain.

When Dave read my poetry he cried and shared my
private hell. I knew this man was more than a friend.
He was the father I so badly needed.

Dave erased a lot of my hurt
and gave me courage to take life on;
he taught me to quit taking foolish chances.

He spoke to me about clean love
and to expect only the best of myself.
This man gave me more than I could ever give.
He had given himself.
I thank him now and always!

Choose to Live

Your anger so real-
you have chosen to let life cheat you-
your illness to beat you.

You had your plans for your happy life
and illness almost stops you boldly.

Continue to love,
have the courage to fight for more time.

Take the time to set your anger aside,
share all your fear, I promise I'll be here.

I need you to want to win this battle,
this war does not only involve you –
it's about everyone who loves you.

Take the now to need me.
Choose to live for you,
your family and your Friends.

My Other Best Friend,
Vivica Miguel

Her quiet demeanor gives a calming effect
to any situation.

She listens with care.

Giving understanding she is my other best friend.

Her heart joyful – God is the center of her life.

Controlling her actions
and emotions she gives love freely.

She lives her faith, her spiritual beauty apparent.

Her high standards and morals are to be exemplified.

She is the pearl of my friendships.

Oh! So present to embellish my heart.

Your Wall

Hurt in your life has caused you to build
a wall around your heart – your barriers are real.

Are you afraid to get close?
Are you avoiding love?

Friendship is the best gift in the world.
You receive love, respect, understanding
and a laughter that dances in your being.

Give yourself this wonderful gift.
Open a window to your wall built of steel.
I may want in!

Hard to Read

You call at your convenience,
almost always with a question.

Business brings us together
friendship just the same.

You are like a closed book
that doesn't want to be read –
your pages hard and crisp not easy to turn.

Is it that you want no one to read the fine print?
Do you have too many incomplete sentences
or not enough of a story?

Open the book and let me read a chapter or two.
I dare you to let me be a true friend.

Gorgeous

You look at me with piercing eyes.
Your vocabulary full of charm.
You take my hands in yours and I allow it.
Could it be my attraction to you, you to me?

I give nothing up easy – sex forget it.
Sell myself short – I will not.
I sacrifice everything and nothing if this is meant to be.

Your gorgeous self – my great reward.
And, me your grand prize.

Only time will tell.

Off Key

The noise became quiet-
still enough to put thought into my feelings.
I could feel emotion.
Emotion I don't want to deal with.

You are not what I need, not now.
You are a player and I don't want you to strum me like
a guitar.

I choose to silence the smoothness of your tune –
by giving you a big bad note,
a very off key good-bye!

Angel of Life

My angel has been you, a distant friend you keep me in
your prayer asking God to keep me safe, healthy.

Your prayer list large, your Rosary always near.
Your prayer sincere - you keep me in mind.

You forget my face but not my name.
I'm the activity person you don't forget.
Absent I am, far I am not.

I treasure your prayer because God shows me you care.
The things that take place in my life are better
because of you.
An angel of life.

Thank you, special prayer, this your gift to me.
You are a special friend BOBO!

In Friendship
For Pattie English, R.N.

The friendship you extended came as a gift.
You opened your heart and home to me
as if I were one of your own.

Your willing spirit ready to embrace my conflicted soul.
Never judging or questioning my mistakes.
This is more than I'd gotten from home.

What you offered was harbor – what I found was love.

Arms Wide Open

Arms wide open, I extend myself to you.
I allow myself to be vulnerable.
In my glory I am open to the thought of love.

Arms wide open, I could be comfortable in your arms.
I would treasure your days well spent with me.

With arms wide open, I believe God has a plan for me.
The gift of a decent, honest man with a spiritual sense
of direction – yes in my direction too!

With arms wide open, I look forward to our meeting
soon to come.

Introductions of hope, a friendship of truth,
a destination finally arrived.

FINDING MY DIRECTION

*The silver lining to life
I irradiate all my gifts of His blessings*

In the Spirit of God

In the Spirit of God I found my way.
The light over powers of my once dark world.
The hope of now carries me through life.

In the Spirit of God I have direction,
a place to be somewhere to go.
To help the less fortunate,
to share my grief.

In the Spirit of God, I hold you now.
You are not alone.
Reach out and I'll take you and show you peace.

Love is a gift,
not to mean a beating or disrespect of a tongue.
Your broken spirit can survive in the Spirit of God.

In His Arms

In His arms the crying stops, the soothing begins.
Calm settles my day, comfort speaks without words.

In His extended arms, I find myself at ease.
I dare to be free to feel the way of His love,
I take it and lather in it.

In His arms I find knowledge of all that is beautiful
and right.
He assures my mind.
I think positive.
I dare to dream.
This gives me much peace and contentment.

In His arms I feel love in its purest form.
The Lord holds me now.
With his Godly embrace holding me close and pushing
me to live His way.
In His arms I have found it all.

Identity

Who in the hell do you think you are?
Gone for ten years and you think I'm dying to see you.

Who in the world do you think I am?
I'll tell you this: I'm not the stupid girl who needed you
so desperately a long time ago.

She is long gone!
She (I) found her identity without you.

Empty? No, Half Dead? Yes

My heart has never been empty.
I have the gift of love; to give, give, and give –
keeping love for myself at a distance.

For love to be present in my life, meant half dead.
Rotten love soils my own need of love.
I reject it, I look away, and I run half dead.

Half dead meant breathing with no purpose;
having no cause.
Loving the wrong; tolerating shame.
Ugly secrets, big hurts, and married to sin.

Half dead – I am no longer.
I breathe with purpose – new direction.
With much life to be lived, I go into a promise of love –
my gift to myself.

A Vision of Hope

A vision of hope appeared for me who had no clear
picture for my future.
It was this day like a puzzle that gave promise of
completeness.

A vision of hope of God's plan in my spiritual life.
Love would come in many forms.
It is His vision for me that has me here today.

A vision of forth to move forward.
To leave old baggage behind, and carry only butterflies.
To throw the weight of the world away.

This vision, so real I can reach out and almost touch it.
Love awaits me, to be taken into strong arms and held
forever.

His vision leaves me with questions:
Who are you?
When will we be?

Will you carry His vision too?

After the Pain

After the pain; comes much life.
Serenity moves in slowly, understanding of a past life
settles, staking its claim.
With friendship comes much love.

After the pain, I come back to life.
I dig into my work, finding much joy.
My heart happy more than fulfilled.

After the pain, comes my spiritual healing.
I am strong now, with a meaning of life.
I release all that held me to the memories
that once hurt me.

God directs me to go forward.
He shows me I am loved by Him and others.
After the pain, I find myself free.

Direction

My direction is straight ahead.
No STOP signs. No DETOURS.
I follow the direction of your choosing to find more
than peace.

The direction you gave was real;
it was an adventure into unknown territory.
I wasn't accustomed to the danger signs being gone.

What I found instead was your huge welcome sign,
as if hung just for me.

Thank you for being oh so powerfully present in my life
and for simple direction.

The Hands of God

Hope found in the extended hand of a stranger.
Love at my receiving end always hurt.
My lack of understanding led me to a dark place.
I seemed to be in a dark hole more than I care to
remember.

I found hope in the extended hands
of many pulling me out of darkness.
All willing to show me the decent way of the world.

Changing my direction;
giving much light far into my future.
I believe they were the hands of God.
I was just too lost to realize it then.

Breaking Ground

Breaking ground didn't come easy.
This foundation I stand on today
wasn't always sitting even.
I felt the uneven ground under my feet.

I prayed for structure –
I got walls to keep me safe inside.
I prayed for cover –
soon came a roof.

I needed color –
He provided friendship with the contractors.
I needed a garden –
there I found serenity.

I had broken ground and found myself efflorescent!

With Understanding

With understanding I know how I came to be.
I learned my destination through you.
I gave my love where it would be noticed.
To those who would appreciate my giving compassion.

I touch the lives of the elderly –
usually widows and forgotten men –
their lives fuller because I care.
My heart overfilled with joy;
they give back more than they know.

They are the grandparents I no longer have.
They are my driving force –
like family who wants only the best for me.
They have adopted me with much compassion.
They are the nutrients of my life.

Taking My Life Back

If I'd paid attention to what I needed,
instead of what I thought he needed,
all this pain would not even exist.

I'm not sure all this blame is his, I have to share it.
I have to claim it – God knows I own it.
It has kept me from loving again –
kept me from trusting men.

I'm taking my life back so I can run and jump
into my days ahead.
I want to shake my heart back into action,
So I'll be ready for life at its fullest.

Illusage

Rewinding my past, moving forward
with tears of joy.

Lessons Learned

Lessons learned came by surprise.
In a slap or a kick,
I found out I had strength to endure.
With the pulling of my hair,
I learned my head had better use.

Through battle,
I learned of peace later on in life.
I searched for it in need of change.
Change for me brought alone with my thoughts.
I found myself happy at last.

Too Much to Ask?

Would it be too much to ask of you to make love to
me as if you are still in love with me?
I need you to hold me as if I still matter some to you.

Lying here in bed feeling alone with you, I feel your
absence although you are lying here next to me.

How good did you feel while on top of me thrusting all
your masculinity in to my body?
How empty do you think I feel with your back to me
as if I were invisible?

Would it be too much to ask of all I need to
understand?

Variety

Making love with you, feeling connected to all that's
going on this moment.
We'd spend our day in bliss, ever happy.
Variety of enjoyment would come to play.

Passion that one reads about exists here and now.
Lustful moments with genuine love.
Variety would be with us –
you needed it and I was willing.

In marriage we gave our promises:
to love, honor and be true.
Variety was with us –
your need for variety was deeper than I knew.
Variety brought women into our bed.

His Words

He arrived in a mood,
smelling of booze, looking crazed.
He had something to announce; he'd met a girl,
he said "I don't need you; don't want you;
I have another to replace you."

I sat there on the porch a bit confused but not surprised.
He'd been with every loose woman in town.
He made no sense, he told me to leave my own home.
When I refused he took his foot and kicked me
in my groin.
It was as if he was trying to knock me out of the chair.

He needed to hurt me, what he didn't realize was that
he'd already hurt me with those first words spoken
straight to my heart.

The kick of his foot would leave a bruise and be gone,
but his words would sit around forever.

Looking In

Looking in from the outside, I see myself crying often,
my eyes very sad.
He has me by my hair – yelling;
he has saved all his rage for me.
This morning he loved me and held me as if I were
more than the rag doll I feel like now.

My tears – real; my fear – big;
and my safety – gone in a blink of an eye.
Looking in, I want to grab myself and run.
How can I grab myself when I am living it? – looking in
from the outside as if spirit and body are divided.

I'm loosing my breath.
My heart pounding hard against my chest.
I fight, but he's to strong for me.
I'm on the floor; bleeding –
I wonder if this is the death of me?
She grabs me and runs as if spirit, heart and soul meet to
keep me alive.

Here I am ever so thankful for the strength in the girl in
me who took me and ran.

Crumbled

The death of my soul was real.
I had been abused so much I couldn't think or eat,
I could barely breathe.

I had spent a decade closing doors,
saying no too many of life's opportunities.
I had a closed mind, and unwilling heart.
Working myself so hard I wouldn't miss the men who
took my being and tore it like paper to be crumbled
and thrown in to the trash.

Private Viewing

If I could replay my young life to show you
how dark depression can be –
I'd give you a private viewing.

You would need a box of tissue
for those eyes that would surely cry.
You would experience my near death times,
when I thought I never mattered.

My struggles were real; I had so little hope
of making it through another day,
I was suicidal;
out of control.
I had no direction,
nowhere to hide,
bleak was everywhere;
it was who I was.

I found that alcohol made everything worse;
men who loved me briefly,
who hurt me more than I hurt myself,
bad love threw me to the curb,
and I foolishly jumped out of a moving car.

Don't play with depression,
you'll find out that it will play with you
and if you let it,
it will win.

Box

Living imprisoned in a box;
short supply of friends; all social activities cut short.
Low on financial resources; forced to quit my work.
Empty of self worth, his chosen words enforce my lack
of value.

Living inside of this box gave him control.
I had no freedom to come or go.
Ugly secrets ours, the shame all mine to bare.
I dying deep inside;
daily I secretly cry with questions of why?

Living inside this box
does little to make me happy just to be.
I hunger to be free of misery;
dare to wonder beyond now.
Today I fell to the floor in prayer asking for help that
I'd find my life outside this box.

Broke, alone, empty, emotionally confused,
I had one thing he'd never have;
my hope of being outside of his box.

Tears of Joy

Thoughts surface a realization
that prayers have been answered.
Tranquility parked in my heart
as if it belongs there.

The meter of life never runs out.
Tears of joy remind me so.

An Abused Persons Prayer
For The Fresh Start Women's Center

Today, I will give thanks that you are alive.
I will pray for you to have strength to change
your situation.

I pray that love does not keep you in chains to anyone.
I pray for you to have courage to walk away.
May you find the light to happiness that will lead to a
door knob that leads you to peace.

I will ask God to open the door of opportunity.
I'll pray that He speaks to your heart,
so you will know that love should never hurt.

Most of all I want you to find
His love and all its meaning.
I'll pray for you today and tomorrow,
just like someone prayed for me.

A Final Thought

You sit with my life in your hands, poetry from my heart in your mind. Flipping these pages with interest knowing abuse is near: you, a friend, or a family member dealing with this awful epidemic. I hope you will be able to complete the chapter of your own life with a beautiful ending.

I hope I have planted inspiration in your life. I pray for you now and always.

"Fresh Start supports women seeking to change their lives by helping them to help themselves"

602.252.8494

Copyright © 2005 Debrah Marlene
Printed in the U.S.A.

Publishing services provided by:
Hispanic Institute of Social Issues
PO Box 50553; Mesa, Arizona 85208-0028
www.hisi.org   (480) 983-1445